بِسْمِ اللّٰهِ الرَّحْمٰنِ الرَّحِيمِ

In the Name of Allah
the Most Gracious the Most Merciful

Beyond Martyrdom
The significance of Imam Hussein and Ashura
Sayyed Abbass Noureddine

ISBN 978-614-474-124-5
First Edition

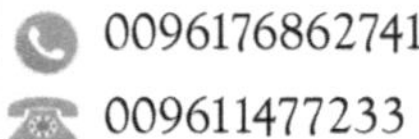

0096176862741
009611477233

BEYOND MARTYRDOM

The Significance of Imam Hussein and Ashura

Sayyed Abbass Noureddine

Translated by:
Mohammad Ali & Amal Abdallah

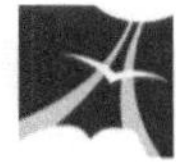

Beit-Al-Kateb Publication

Table of Contents

Introduction

In the Name of Allah, the Most Gracious, the Most Merciful.

Peace be upon you O' Abu Abdullah, and upon the souls that have gathered in your sanctuary...

Indeed, the martyrdom of Hussein ignites a flame in the hearts of the faithful, a heat that will never extinguish.

Imam Hussein bin Ali, the grandson of the greatest Prophet, peace be on them all, is present in the conscience of every believer who loves Islam and adores the Prophet (p). How could he not, when all the virtue and dignity we relish in our lives stem from the benevolent Prophet who rescued us from the verge of perdition and damnation.

A believer does not require reminders to recall the Prophet, for their life revolves around this great man.

He forms an inseparable part of our of prayers to such extent that without his remembrance there is no prayer; this prayer which is the soul of our lives, the pulse of our hearts, the sign of our existence and our connection to the wellspring of goodness, joy, emanation, life and perfection.

Every breath, feeling, heartbeat, and movement we make stem from the Holy Prophet (p) and his family (a.s.). This is an undeniable truth.

Imam Hussein, the apple of the Prophet's eye, shares an inseparable bond with him. Hussein is from the Prophet and the Prophet is from him. Thus, it is impossible to think about the Prophet without thinking about his martyred grandson, who offered the greatest sacrifice ever to safeguard everything the Prophet held dear. Prophet Mohammad (p) who totally devoted himself to the Message, and whose sole goal was the revival of humanity through this Message, stands as the symbol of Islam, faith, survival, and salvation in this life and the hereafter. Imam Hussein, by shedding his pure blood, upheld this Message, ensuring its guiding light endures through the ages. Thus, while the Prophet was the founder, Imam Hussein was the guardian.

To envisage a world without Imam Hussein, we need only look to the unparalleled atrocities perpetrated by Yazid and his cohorts against Muslims in a matter of mere years. This tyrant was merely completing what his father had initiated eradicating every trace of the Prophet out of thirst for revenge borne from their humiliating defeats in the battles of Badr and Uhud, a thirst which poisoned their already corrupt, fanatic, and malevolent hearts! This brutal spree went largely unnoticed by Muslims, who had lost their resolve. Then, Imam Hussein emerged like a magnificent boulder, a towering mountain blocking the path of a hurtling train! This was the jolt that made Yazid and his followers lose their composure, as they came to the hard realization that their dream to exterminate Islam and erase the Prophet's name was beyond their reach.

Had this nation heeded Imam Hussein's call in earnest, the accursed tree referred to in the Quran would have been uprooted instantly. But, the community stood at the brink of another trial; a trial that would expose the inner recesses of their souls and lay the foundation for faith, because faith cannot exist untested: "Do the people suppose that they will be let off because they say, 'We have faith,' and they will not be tested?"[1]

Silence neither nurtures faith nor builds nations. Only a nation that is alive, active, willing to make sacrifices, and resolute can bring glory to its citizens. The day will undoubtedly come when this nation will be united under the banner of Islam and its lofty moral values. Then, Imam Hussein will return. And just as his initial uprising quelled the tyrants' plans, he will again be the catalyst for the revival and renaissance of nations, rendering them the noblest, most progressive, and prosperous of all.

Yet, all of this is contingent on the level of public awareness. Consider then, if the mere flicker of awareness during Ashura and its aftermath was enough to thwart the Umayyad plans, then what if this awareness grows and deepens, and the grand lessons and principles of the uprising of Imam Hussein - the role model for every freedom seeker - uprising are fully comprehended?!

Back then, the mere recognition of Imam Hussein's murder as a grave assault against Prophet Mohammad would have been enough for a Muslim to denounce Yazid's reign and his followers, rejecting the multitude of falsehoods and pretenses that enveloped them. Yet, today we have the opportunity to delve deeper and gain a more profound understanding of Imam Hussein's objectives and the true essence of his reform movement. 

At every opportunity, the faithful reflect on the events of Ashura - their implications, principles, and objectives - and pose significant questions to unravel its secrets. In turn, the uprising continually provides us with restorative answers and guiding wisdom, illuminating our lives and pathways, helping us to perceive life and existence in a clearer and more profound way. For this reason, Imam Hussein's Karbala stands as an extraordinary institution that ceaselessly cultivates generations, fosters faith, and shapes life. As long as the burning flame in the hearts of the faithful unites them, enlightens their minds, inspires them, and stimulates their potential in the pursuit of global reform, Karbala will remain as such.

Chapter 1

Ashura: An Inspiring Historical Incident

History is not merely a sequence of events that took place in the past. Rather, it serves as a vast canvas revealing to us a critical collection of divine laws. In essence, history is a grand stage where the divine presence comes to life, for nothing in this universe is beyond the reach of Allah's meticulously crafted design and profound wisdom. All worldly occurrences, events and incidents are the handiwork of Allah, shaped by His wisdom and guided by His plan. This overarching rule naturally extends to historical happenings as well. Hence, our exploration of history is driven by the desire to grasp Allah's wisdom and establish a connection with It. This understanding, in turn, will lead us to appreciate the grandeur of Allah, prompting us to confront our own humble existence and relative insignificance. It instills us with a sense of being humble servants in need of Allah's grace. As such, our love for Him will intensify as will our yearning to form a deep and lasting bond with Him. Living a life of servitude, approaching Allah with love and reverence, we foster this connection, through which we partake in the divine effusion and grow in knowledge, wisdom, capability, and perfection.

Therefore, delving into history becomes a path that brings us closer to Allah. As we draw nearer to Him, we gain heightened awareness, insight, and knowledge about the current events and the intricate nuances of our lives. This is the ultimate reward of learning the divine laws of wisdom and the principles that govern the past, present, and future.

An insightful awareness of the present and its unfolding events equips us with foresight to anticipate our future and the trajectory of the world. Thus, we can avoid a myriad of potential errors that may arise when navigating challenges or crises. One such significant mistake lies in the failure to adopt the correct stance when confronted with challenges or neglecting to make the right move at the opportune moment. Such oversight may trigger severe consequences and immense losses, potentially leading to the downfall and disintegration of the individuals or groups committing this error!

As we bear witness to various events today, we acknowledge that many could beget serious future problems or pave the way for our misery and defeat, unless we tackle them as a unified human collective. This is where our reliance on history surfaces. History empowers us to compare past and present events, unveiling that our present is but a mirror of the past. It imparts insights into the fate of people who faced situations akin to ours, and the implications of their responses - perhaps a society surrendered to the rule of a despot, paying the price in forfeited dignity, happiness, and prosperity, akin to the German people under Hitler. A society might also overlook the potential of its geographical location, failing to leverage it for growth and progress. 

The narrative of every extinct civilization underscores that humans shape their destiny at critical junctures, and how they shape it depends on their awareness, understanding of surrounding events and their knowledge of history.

An analogy often drawn is that of a community's life to passengers on a ship. When one passenger begins to bore holes in the ship, the rest can choose to intervene, saving everyone, or remain passive, resulting in a collective demise.

This predicament often recurs in societies where a majority opts for inaction, dismissing issues as irrelevant to them until they witness their society's corruption or destruction.

History abounds with such incidents. A thorough exploration of its vast chronicles uncovers lessons applicable to our era and society, making history an invaluable reservoir of moral lessons, as well as a source of inspiration.

To better understand our present circumstances and future, we turn to history. Which of its numerous events best elucidate our current situation?

In the present day,our society grapples with significant issues and confronts a host of problems and crises. Numerous challenges and external threats loom, some presented by enemies who are intent on our destruction and seizure of our resources. However, we are not the first society to encounter such predicaments.

These experiences recur throughout history. Few societies exist that have not weathered such storms in their social life.

As we look into history for challenges and crises akin to our own or seek a historical incident that enables us to see the reality of things, what emerges is the uprising of Imam Hussein (as), the brilliant beacon that illuminated the tenth of Muharram, casting its radiance across the globe's vast expanses.

> Indeed, Muharram was a month during which the people of the Age of Ignorance prohibited fighting. Yet, in it, our blood was unjustly shed, our sanctity violated, and our progeny and women taken captive. Fires were kindled in our dwellings and our possessions plundered. No respect was shown for the sanctity of the Messenger of Allah in our affairs.
> The day of Hussein has indeed made our eyes overflow with tears, and our hearts bleed. Our noble one was humiliated in the land of tribulation and calamity. This has bequeathed to us sorrow and affliction until the Day of Judgment. So let those who weep, weep for the likes of Hussein, for truly, weeping for him washes away the gravest of sins.[2]
> Imam Rida (as)

Chapter 2

Reaping the Lessons of Ashura

Our Islamic history is full of momentous events and significant turning points, yet one episode continually demands our attention - the incident of Ashura. This moment encapsulates the path of societal and reformation uprising led by Imam Hussein (as), son of Ali (as), grandson of the most honorable Prophet (p), and the cherished light in his eyes.

The incident of Ashura, one of the most widely remembered and impactful historical moments within Islamic society, has ignited the creative imagination of poets, sparked the curiosity of researchers, and shaped the thoughts of thinkers in a way that no other event can rival.

To those familiar with Imam Hussein, it's clear that his uprising aimed to reform society, protect religion, and preserve it against distortion - as he himself declared.

Although Ashura primarily depicted the response of Imam Hussein and his companions to their contemporary conditions, deeper contemplation of this pivotal uprising reveals its enduring capacity to impart powerful lessons — as it has done in the centuries following its occurrence.

Today, Ashura is viewed as a great school rich in ethical teachings and interpretations of significant social and historical laws. In short, it acquaints us with the principles of victory, the prerequisites for triumph, the pathways to success, and the strides towards prosperity. Conversely, it shines light on the element of defeat and the reasons for failure and decay which any society may face.

Chapter 3

Why Is Ashura Regarded as a Principal School of Thought?

Why does pondering and analyzing the incident of Karbala introduce us to all these major social laws? The underlying secret is that this great historical event encapsulated the conflict between absolute faith and absolute falsehood. In a brief period and confined area, it unveiled an intense confrontation between the camp of truth exhibited in its most radiant and profound form and the front of unbelief presented in its harshest and most revolting depiction.

By "intense confrontation" we mean that both sides laid bare their full spectra of faith and unbelief, of beauty and horror, of virtue and vice, as if Ashura became the stage where humanity showed its most sublime possible image (evidenced in the camp of Imam Hussein and the front of truth), and as well as its vilest potential state of wickedness, ugliness and degradation.

In Ashura, the unique grandeur of humanity was witnessed in all its aspects: faith, creed, intellect, morality, behavior, and emotions, embodied in Imam Hussein, the Martyr, and his companions. This event gave them the platform to demonstrate the epitome of human perfection, brilliance, and merit.

Additionally, Ashura shone a light on the devolving humanity steeped in degradation, depravity, savagery, and brutality. It unveiled dismal depths humanity can descend to once separated from faith, humanity, and innate nature (*fitrah*).

In Ashura, Allah wanted us to see perfection and virtue in their most sublime and finest images through their confrontation with their opposites, which is a very helpful means to perceive the reality of things. In Ashura, absolute, pure truth clashed with complete falsehood, with comprehensive faith meeting total unbelief, enabling us to discern each side with crystal clarity.

We were afforded a glimpse of what the perfect human could become, given the opportunity to reveal the full splendor of their spirit, the magnificence of their virtues, and their lofty perfection. Conversely, we saw the horrifying image of a person who has entirely discarded moral restraint, a spectacle worse than that of wild beasts!

Thus, Ashura distinguishes itself from most historical encounters where only fragments of humanity and degrees of virtue and vice are unveiled by being a historical experience that thoroughly uncovers the truth.

Ashura also laid bare the inner workings of the human soul. It exposed the disparate motivations, highlighting the heroism, nobility, and sublimity on one side, and the abhorrent degradation and brutality on the other. The stark contrast left no room for doubt regarding the nature of truth's front and its motivations, or the nature and motivations of those in the front of falsehood. 

All that transpires in our lives or within any society or group is, in essence, a hidden struggle between truth and falsehood. No event can illustrate this conflict, its repercussions, and fruits more vividly than Imam Hussein's uprising.

So, whenever we seek to comprehend the underpinnings of our life's, challenges this ongoing battle and confrontation - Ashura stands ready to illuminate and elucidate. Consequently, those who have gleaned wisdom from this significant school of thought can decipher world events and perceive their secrets and outcomes.

The insight, enlightenment, understanding, and wisdom granted by Ashura empower these individuals to comprehend any issue and predict its trajectory and outcome. They emerge as the most profound, aware, and discerning among us.

A shallow person may struggle to interpret societal events,

while an average person might discern some immediate causes. However, a graduate of the school of Karbala can unearth the authentic roots, comprehend the present reality, and envision the future. A true believer perceives that any movement, activity, conflict, or clash is instigated by elements of truth or falsehood, faith or disbelief. This awareness equips them to discern the genuine motivations underlying these events.

"O Dibil anyone who weeps or makes others weep for our affliction, even if it is a single individual, his reward is upon Allah. O Dibil, he who sheds tears for the tragedies we have endured at the hands of our enemies, Allah will resurrect him in our company on the Day of Judgment. O Dibil, he who weeps for the suffering of my grandfather Hussein, Allah will surely forgive all his sins."[3]
Imam Rida (as)

Here, Ashura provides a comprehensive portrayal of the potential outcomes of a confrontation between faith and unbelief, truth and falsehood, virtue and vice. It serves as an exceptional school for understanding humanity and society, for comprehending history, and for perceiving the divine wisdom and grand design.

In life, we often encounter situations where truth appears weakened, diluted by falsehood, and hence they reflect but half-truth. Similarly, we encounter individuals who embody virtue to a limited extent, their good qualities tainted by vices. Some may display diminished faith, having allowed unbelief to infiltrate their hearts. This mix of truth with falsehood, vulnerability, and deficiency often obstruct our recognition of the authentic nature of truth and falsehood, making it challenging to identify virtue in its purest form.

However, understanding how a perfect human confronts

their fiercest enemy, as Ashura elucidates, presents an opportunity to distinguish between truth and falsehood, virtue and vice, and faith and unbelief.

Indeed, many of our life's confrontations aren't strictly between absolute truth and complete falsehood. This is due to issues and deficiencies within the ranks of the faithful and virtuous, concerning their motivations, nature, behavior, and morals. Similarly, the front of falsehood may harbor elements of truth and beauty, adding complexity to understanding the situation and predicting the future.

> "Indeed, the usurper and honerless son of the usurper and honerless has presented me with two options - one of hardship [inadequacy] and the other of humiliation. But, indeed, humiliation is far away from us. Allah refuses it, as do His Messenger and the faithfull. Blessed are my ancestors and pure are their graves. We have dignified countenances and noble souls that refuse to prefer the grazing lands of the base over the grazing lands of the noble."[4]
> Imam Hussein (as)

We might question whether the virtuous can prevail even if they harbor wasteful and extravagant individuals among them. Or despite weaknesses in their spirituality, faith, and etiquette, could they still emerge victorious?

While we understand that their cause is rightful and should triumph, these deficiencies and errors can incite doubt because they introduce elements of falsehood to their otherwise righteous cause.

In contrast, Ashura represented absolute truth, pure virtue, and perfect faith. Each position and stance in Imam Hussein's camp manifested absolute faith and exemplary virtue. It is as if Imam Hussein intended his camp to be pure and untarnished, ready to bestow upon humanity the greatest gift it requires for its journey through life: the knowledge of truth and falsehood, the understanding of faith and disbelief, and the perception of virtue and vice.

While every historical event can enhance our awareness and knowledge of truth and falsehood, faith and unbelief, no incident parallels Ashura in the degree of awareness, insight, knowledge, and wisdom it imparts.

Ashura: The Epitome of Islam

The narrative of Imam Hussein's uprising is not limited to particular occurrences spanning just a few days or months. Instead, it threads back to the dawn of humanity with Adam, and stretches into the future until the rise of Imam Al-Mahdi - may Allah hasten his reappearance - who will bear Imam Hussein's banner and echo his call: "O' Hussein, I am at your service!"

As such, comprehending all the aspects of Imam Hussein's uprising, which has fueled the creativity of authors, poets, scholars, and orators for centuries, cannot be achieved through a mere handful of writings. Ashura is the school that encapsulated the entirety of Islam, mirroring this noble religion in its truest form. Grasping its profound implications requires more than a cursory glance – it demands the dedication of a skilled explorer who patiently delves into its depths, rather than settling for fragments and mistaking them for the whole.

Following the death of Prophet Mohammad, interpretations and explanations proliferated, giving rise to numerous schools of thought, currents, and sects within the Islamic world. Each claimed hold of the essence of true religion, citing verses from the Quran and hadiths as proof. Yet, the vast discrepancies among these factions signaled that most did not truly embody the essence of Islam. As Imam Ali (as) stated, "Whenever two calls conflict, one of them is assuredly in error." Prophet Mohammad foresaw the turmoil that would cloud the true path of Islam following his departure, despite the preservation of religious teachings.

In the five decades after the Prophet's death, Islamic teachings and laws continued to guide the Islamic community. However, what was lost was not the teachings or the laws themselves, but the path and spirit of Islam. This loss birthed a multitude of religious interpretations that left behind only an external semblance of Islam.

The true existence of Islam is gauged by the degree to which it is embodied in people's lives, not merely preserved in the Quran and hadiths. Hence, knowing the path and defending it are of paramount importance, representing the greatest honor and privilege in life.

The Holy Quran and the Prophet's hadiths depict Islam as an accessible religion - easy, facilitated, and imbued with a lenient sharia, providing a clear path towards Allah. So, where is this guiding light that illuminates each moment of our lives? What is this beacon that reveals the essence of the perfect human being and aids us in realizing it? Which path did the Prophet intend for us to follow after his departure?

The Prophet entrusted his followers with a mission - Jihad. As he said, "Indeed, every nation has a journey and the journey of my nation is Jihad in the way of Allah." Aware of the trials his nation would face, he pointed out the guiding light that would illuminate the way, saying, "Hussein is from me and I am from Hussein." Thus, anyone seeking to follow the Prophet must seek "his" Hussein.

Hussein is the beacon of guidance and the ark of salvation.

Chapter 4

Who Benefits from Ashura?

Muslims unanimously recognize the events of Ashura, which took place on the 10th of Muharram, 61 AH. This day marked the tragic martyrdom of Prophet Mohammad's (p) grandson, along with his household and companions. His surviving family, which also constituted Prophet Mohammad's family, were taken as captivates.

Muslims also agree that Hussein (as), son of Ali and Fatima Al-Zahra - the daughter of the Messenger of Allah (p) - rose in rebellion against the ruling authority.

Despite the magnitude of this historical event, a significant segment of Muslims has shown little interest in it. Some view discussions of Ashura as irrelevant, advocating for the detachment from the past with the reasoning, "That was a nation that has passed: for it there will be what it has earned, and for you there will be what you have earned, and you will not be questioned about what they used to do."[6] Additionally, others perceive discussions, contemplation, research, or reading about this event as potentially reigniting old wounds and stirring discord among Muslims, saying that any reference to this event can hurt the feelings of some or embarrass others. Nevertheless, by neglecting such a critical chapter of Islamic history, they deprived themselves of a comprehensive understanding of that history, its influence on the Islamic call, and the divine message. They inadvertently robbed themselves of the opportunity to fully comprehend present events and grasp many divine and historical laws that govern the fate of societies and nations. Consequently, they lost the chance to discern the appropriate stance concerning major incidents and issues in their lives.

To appreciate the importance of Ashura and its position, it is crucial to understand what we mean by Islamic history.

Islamic history isn't merely a collection of independent

events or the history of a specific group or individuals. Instead, it is a single prolonged movement – a continuum of realities and missionary events initiated and led by Prophet Mohammad (p) throughout his noble life before passing the torch to his successor. Removal of a single link in this chain alters, indeed shatters, history, causing the truth to be lost.

Before the honorable Mission, the world was moving in a direction or along a path described by the Holy Quran as: "And you were on the brink of a pit of Fire, whereat He saved you from it."[7] Humanity was spiraling towards the bottom of Hell, represented in this world in the image of corruption, despair, misery, and suffering. However, the Messenger of Allah (p) came forth and altered the trajectory of human history. He paved a new path for humanity towards heaven, happiness, wellbeing, sublime values, virtue, and all that is beautiful. This path, once established, drew a group of followers who supported and aided the Prophet until it was firmly established for all of humanity. This alternative path invited people from around the world to pursue happiness in this life, honor in the afterlife, and secure their security, pride, and prosperity. 

The inception of this call marked the beginning of the struggle between the divine message and its adversaries. This struggle, due to the potency of the social movement led by Prophet Mohammad and its great influence, became a significant factor in shaping the course of history and the fate of peoples.

The confrontation that began with the call to Allah and Islam became the central pivot around which all major incidents following the honorable message revolved.
People worldwide were divided into factions and became part of this confrontation, either directly or indirectly, closely or distantly. No corner of the world was untouched

by the Islamic Message movement, as every society played a role - as a supporter, observer, bystander, opposer, or enemy. Every event following the Prophet's death, especially within the primary circle of interaction (the society from which Prophet Mohammad launched his call), was focused on preserving this movement and maintaining the path that he opened to all humanity.

> "A group from my community will claim to belong to my faith. They will murder the most virtuous of my progeny and the purest of my lineage. They will alter my laws and my traditions. They will kill my sons Hassan and Hussein, just as the ancestors of these Jews killed Zechariah and John. Indeed, Allah will curse them just as He cursed them. And before the Day of Resurrection, He will raise a rightly-guiding redeemer from the oppressed progeny of Hussein will burn them with the swords of his loyalties all the way to hell.
> Prophet Mohammad[8]

Therefore, humanity was given a promise of a future, currently being shaped within the crucible of this confrontation.

Chapter 5

How people interacted with the Message

Since the emergence of the Prophet's Message, humanity's response has taken various forms. One faction has vehemently opposed this message, striving to obliterate or distort its righteous path, unaware of the profound implications of their actions. Others have chosen to tread its path, albeit without fully appreciating its vital importance to their lives. Their adherence was driven by personal interest or serendipity; they found themselves reaping certain benefits along this path.

Only a minuscule segment of people consciously chose this path. These insightful individuals recognized the underlying dynamics, grasped the core principles, foresaw the direction of unfolding events, understood the interlinked chain of history, and kept their gaze fixed on the future and the culmination of this confrontation.

It is through the lens of history that we discern these categories as we explore the struggle between truth and falsehood that has been evident since the inception of the honorable Mission.

A discerning reader of Islamic history realizes that it represents a sequence of interconnected and successive events. Every encounter between the righteous and the purveyors of falsehood along this path has served as a prelude to subsequent confrontations. Each clash between the two camps has laid the groundwork for future conflicts and shaped them. This is precisely the concept encapsulated by the term "succession of events" in Islamic history.

Every battle waged in any corner of the Islamic world, or any stance adopted by a group of Muslims, can trace its origins back to the dawn of the Islamic call. The Mission was akin to an explosion whose echoes reverberated throughout history, these echoes manifesting as diverse stances taken by people wherever they resided.

Consider, for example, the battle of Badr, which occurred in the second year after Hijra.

If we regard this as one of the many confrontations between the two camps, we see how the actions, performance, and stances of the faithful set in motion a chain of events and repercussions, significantly influencing future confrontations, whether they were battles or not. Each confrontation, in turn, led to new consequences and precipitated a fresh conflict. This is how historical events have intertwined, starting from the initial event.

We know that humanity has not yet reached the end of the path established by the Prophet (p), nor have the fruits of this path fully ripened. People continue to tread this road, either as proponents and supporters, or as adversaries and observers.

Rather than progressing along this path, humanity is still caught up in conflict over the path itself.

Allah said, "If they are steadfast on the path [of Allah], We shall provide them with abundant water."[9]

In contemporary discourse, Western states repeatedly

> "When Muawiya passed away and his son Yazid assumed power... He said, ‹The Commander of the Faithful commands you to pledge allegiance to him.› To this, Hussein, peace be upon him, replied, ‹O Utbah, you know well that we are the family of honor, the source of prophethood, and the bearers of truth. Allah the Almighty has entrusted our hearts with this and made our tongues fluent in it, allowing us to speak by His permission. I heard my grandfather, the Messenger of Allah, peace be upon him and his progeny, say that the Caliphate is forbidden to the sons of Abu Sufyan. How then can I pledge allegiance to a house about which the Messenger of Allah, peace be upon him and his progeny, has made such a statement?›"
> Imam Al-Sadiq(a)[10]

characterize Islam as a primary threat. You are likely aware that the major global conflicts are occurring within Islamic societies. Yet, this path remains steadfast, despite such animosity and fierce confrontations.

While the Messenger of Allah's call to humanity and his glad tidings of a virtuous, prosperous, and perfect society, as well as the establishment of religion on earth, has not yet fully materialized, people still have the ability to discern the right path that leads to happiness, prosperity, and sublimity.

Mysticism(Irfan) and Martyrdom

One might think that martyrdom is an arduous path when compared to other paths like preaching, giving charity, or performing other virtuous deeds, and hence if given the choice won't take such path, for it is a path marked by combat, challenges, and enormous sacrifice. Yet, in truth, martyrdom is far more profound than it appears on the surface. It is a door that, though torturous on the exterior, reveals boundless mercy within. It is, indeed, the swiftest and most resolute path to take.

Prophet Mohammad spent twenty-three years delivering the message of Islam. Yet, Imam Hussein, through his immortal martyrdom, managed to preserve and rejuvenate this message in a single day. He encapsulated a journey spanning more than two decades into one day; rather, into a few hours!

Jihad which people often view unfavorably, is a gate that Allah has opened for His most cherished followers. As Imam Ali (as) expressed, "Indeed, jihad is a gateway that God has opened exclusively for His chosen allies."[11] Therefore, imagine the sanctity of martyrdom, which is bestowed upon the most esteemed among the favored! Imam Hussein endured and condensed the trials associated with death to safeguard religion, imploring us to rush towards him and join him, stating "Whoever joins us will be martyred and whoever does not will not attain victory." So, what exactly is the prize to be conquered? Is it territorial gains!? Or is it the most valuable conquest of all!?

Mystics (*Urafa*) suggest that in one's spiritual journey, there's a need to depart from the confines of the soul. The pilgrimage towards Allah necessitates a migration: "And whoever leaves his home migrating toward Allah and His Apostle..."[12]

Before Prophet Mohammad (p), all prophets and their most devout followers undertook this migration towards Allah. However, with the advent of Prophet Mohammad, the migration evolved to a journey towards Allah and His Prophet, underscoring the unique and distinguished nature of Prophet Mohammad's path.

Migration necessitates a sense of urgency, a sense of racing towards the destination. "Hasten towards your Lord's forgiveness", "Hasten towards all that is good" . In Islam, such haste and precedence are achievable only through martyrdom. Yet, martyrdom is not restricted to falling in battle. Some martyrs are slain by adversaries, while others could be considered as living martyrs who, if asked to surrender their lives, would do so immediately and without hesitation. This is the true embodiment of a martyr and a mystic (*arif*). A true mystic is the one who severs earthly attachments. Therefore, authentic mysticism, or Irfan, is deeply intertwined with the concept of martyrdom.

Chapter 6

Ashura: The Bastion of the Path

Regarded as one of the seminal confrontations subsequent to the honorable Mission, Ashura shines as a beacon, the second most pivotal landmark in Islamic history. What elevates Ashura above countless other significant confrontations and advancements in the interim between the Mission and Imam Hussein's uprising, is its encapsulation and distillation of Islamic tenets and values. It assumed an instrumental role in safeguarding the path of the Message, illuminating its purpose for all of humanity.

The illustrious accomplishments achieved post the honorable Mission did not preclude Ashura from obtaining its deserved stature and worth. It emerged as the most fertile source of moral lessons and examples associated with this confrontation along Islam's path. This is primarily because it encompassed all categories and groups of people. Though geographically and temporally confined, it laid bare the positions of the truth-front supporters of the Message, as well as the falsehood-front within the expansive Islamic society. It reoriented both parties; the adherents of the Message and its adversaries were realigned to their rightful places in this significant confrontation.

Regarding the other civilizations coexisting during that time, such as the Romans, Indians, Sindhis and others, they were largely passive observers, not directly engaged. Had the Islamic society's situation been resolved then, and the internal conflict ceased, the truth and falsehood confrontation would have shifted to these civilizations, subsequently clarifying the path and dividing them into two primary groups: the truth faction and the falsehood faction.

A confrontation between truth and falsehood does not inherently imply combat and bloodshed. Many confrontations post the Mission were devoid of bloodshed, battles, or swordplay. They were instead clashes of words, with poetry, debate, and discourse sometimes proving more impactful than physical combat. Nevertheless, historians often overlook these non-violent confrontations, drawn more to the spectacles of louder actions.

"I bear witness that those who opposed you and waged war against you, those who abandoned you and those who killed you are cursed, as declared by the unlettered Prophet. Indeed, those who forged lies have failed. May Allah curse the wrongdoers among you, both the first and the last, and may He inflict upon them a painful torment, redoubled."[15]
Imam Al-Sadiq (as)

Therefore, Ashura represents a vibrant encapsulation of the events that unfolded in the Islamic world since the beginning of the Call. The Islamic world then was a tapestry of cultures extending from North Africa to the fringes of Iran, with Arabs forming its majority demographically. That's why the majority of the confrontations unfolded among them, primarily in its three capital cities located in Hijaz, Iraq, and Sham. Over time, Hijaz receded, and its influence waned. Thus, the Islamic world's epicenter was split between Iraq and Sham, the two venues where the Ashura conflict was anticipated to transpire.

Chapter 7

The Pivotal Clash of Ashura

To fully grasp the significance of the monumental event that Ashura represents, we must first trace the genesis and evolution of the conflict between the devotees of the Message and their adversaries. From the moment Prophet Mohammad initiated his call to Islam, he encountered stringent opposition from his own people and fierce defiance from the surrounding Arab tribes. Nonetheless, Allah fortified and guided him with a select band of believers who, despite their humble numbers, proved to be of substantial influence. Increasingly, individuals began to align, motivated by various factors, such as personal ambition, fear of the growing strength and power of Muslims, or simple greed.

Among these greedy or fearful people, there were those who were known for their hypocrisy and tainted hearts. They had not truly believed in Islam nor embraced it out of conviction. Aware of their true nature, Prophet Mohammad chose to engage with them based on a fundamental principle. He saw their embracing of Islam as a crucial opportunity to disseminate the religion and fortify its path. The principle at work aimed to create an environment conducive to emotional and psychological transformation, giving the chance for the hypocrites and those with tainted hearts to discover the profound and spiritual richness of Islam, inciting an internal change.

In order to foster such a virtuous community, the Prophet placed his trust in individuals who epitomized the highest degrees of faith and adhered unerringly to the pure principles of Islam.

Once this core group of devout believers solidified their stance, the archetypal Islamic community would be established, thus verifying and fortifying the path of the Mission as a testament to the worlds.

However, should this endeavor fail, and the vanguard of true believers fail to present an exemplary experience, the weaker and hypocrite factions could potentially become antagonistic towards Islam and its message, manifesting the same hostility as non-believers and pagans.

This treachery would be even more perilous due to their knowledge of the inner workings of the believers and their points of strengths, which they could exploit to their advantage, concealing the beauty of Islam and the grandeur of its message while presenting a disfigured image of faith.

These dissidents were an anticipated part of the conflicts and confrontations within the Arab community, marking a significant vulnerability and threat. However, this weakness could be transformed into a strength if the faithful were successful in converting these hypocrites into sincere believers, contingent entirely upon the construction of an appropriate nurturing environment.

So, what constitutes the primary factor in this Islamic educational environment? Why were the early Muslims unable to establish this atmosphere, despite their immense sacrifices and jihad, leading to the eventual betrayal by the hypocrites who seized control of the Islamic society?

From the onset, the early believers and the faithful followers of the Message were required to battle on two fronts: the external front against non-believers and pagans, and the internal front contending with the hypocrites and those with tainted hearts.

The external front demanded direct combat due to the infidels' defiance. Accordingly, the believers managed to achieve significant results in record time, beating the infidels and polytheists in the early stages, eventually demolishing their government and sovereignty in the Arabian Peninsula. However, dealing with the hypocrites and the internal confrontation was more severe and difficult, and it required additional elements of jihad, the believers did not possess. As a result, they failed to foster the appropriate environment to transform the hypocrites following the Prophet's passing. The aftermath was devastating, with the hypocrites infiltrating the state's divisions, corrupting the faith experience, seizing control of key Islamic power centers, and ultimately projecting a twisted representation of the Message, as was the case in Sham.

When matters deteriorated to such a degree, it became difficult for people, especially outsiders, to discern the authentic path set by the Prophet. Suppose you were an Italian resident during this time, journeying to the Islamic society to study the Islamic call and learn about the new social movement and its representatives. The true representatives would have been elusive, and instead, a counterfeit path would have been presented as the true Islamic path. Amid conflicting claims of adherence to Islam, discerning truth from falsehood would have been a formidable task, not achievable but with special divine mercy. The pretentious hypocrites soon reached a very dangerous stage. They dominated most areas in the Islamic society, and had the upper hand in that internal confrontation. What was more dangerous was that their actions concealed the path of Islam and distorted humanity's salvation path.

This is the societal backdrop leading up to the uprising of Imam Hussein. He was the third to assume leadership of this internal confrontation, after his brother, Imam Hassan Al-Mujtaba, and his father Imam Ali, the successor of the original leader, Prophet Mohammad (p).

Prophet Muhammad (peace be upon him) announced to the early believers that he had no fear for Islam from the infidels and its external enemies, because God would suppress them with their disbelief, nor he had any fear from the true believers, because God would restrain them by their faith. Yet the only fear he had was from the hypocrites - those who wore the mask of deceit and spoke with a forked tongue.

> "Do you not see that truth is not acted upon, and falsehood is not refrained from? Thus, the believers should desire the meeting with Allah, the Almighty and Glorious. For indeed, I see death as nothing but happiness, and life with the unjust oppressors as nothing but distress."[16]
> Imam Hussein (as)

Imam Ali was the commander of the faithful during this conflict between truth and falsehood along Islam's path. He led the charge in both the internal and external confrontations.

He emerged victorious over the non-believers, as showcased in the battles of Badr, Khaybar, and Al-Ahzab, effectively undermining their might. Yet, in the internal battle, due to the weaknesses within the believers' front and their inability to comprehend the nature and prerequisites of the struggle (the issue of divine imamate being paramount), Imam Ali was beset with a succession of calamities. These adverse events led to the encirclement and isolation of the faithful, allowing the hypocrites to seize control over the Islamic society.

The Path of Imam Hussein

The divine trust, an entity of profound significance, was handed over by Allah to a succession of prophets. Each prophet endeavored to guard this trust with unwavering determination and vigor until the Day of Judgement. Yet, previous prophets were unable to secure the sanctity of this trust, or maintain the integrity of their preached faith from being tainted or utterly lost after their death. This led to the disappearance of the clear path and laws, as stated, "For each [community] among you We had appointed a code [of law] and a path."[17]

This occurred for numerous reasons, one being the immense burden of carrying the divine message and preserving it until the Day of Judgement demanded a degree of sacrifice and fortitude that only the most honored Prophet (p) could shoulder.

The path of the Prophet is encapsulated in his words: "I am from Hussein and Hussein is from me"; a phrase carrying a hidden secret that needs exploration.

To maintain the authenticity of a religion, a personality embodying the entirety of its tenets and dimensions is required. Perceiving religion as merely phrases and terms found within books is a fruitless endeavor, obscuring the essence of what truly preserving a faith means. A religion's preservation calls for a figure equivalent in depth and strength to the religion itself, acting as a bulwark against misinterpretation and distortion. Religion transcends mere verbal teachings; its reality is deeply rooted in the persona of the Prophet himself. The Prophet's persona and its manifestations serve as the path and the Shari'a. By the Prophet's law or Shari'a we mean the Prophet's words, actions, and seal of approval. Therefore, the longevity, vigor and permanence of a religion are intricately tied to those same qualities in its bearer, if the prophet cannot find a successor who embodies these traits, his path and laws are doomed to fade.

Prophet Mohammad nurtured his successor to reflect his attributes and virtues. The Prophet laid the foundations, and the responsibility of preserving the path from being lost and making it accessible for people was passed on to the Imams. Imam Hussein symbolized this responsibility by embracing the path of martyrdom. He condensed the trials and tribulations, the tragedies and obstacles of a journey towards Allah, typically spread over years, into a single act and in a single day. That is what Imam Hussein (as) did.

Chapter 8

The Frailty of the Faithful's Front

It is undeniable that the characteristics and actions of the faithful, such as their awareness, sincerity, stability, and adherence to the principles of Islam, influenced the strength of the faith community, and subsequently, the progress of its establishment.

Judging by historical accounts, it appears the faithful were not as steadfast, sincere, insightful, generous, and sacrificial as they should have been. Hence, any confusion or failures in presenting the path of Islam can be attributed to their shortcomings. However, they also deserve recognition for any advancements or accomplishments as well as for illuminating the path of Islam through their jihad, sacrifices, and dignity.

In sum, despite all the failures, hurdles, and threats posed by infidels, deniers, hypocrites, and those with unsound hearts, the jihad and sacrifices of this devout and proactive group of believers successfully safeguarded the path of Islam.

Chapter 9

Establishing the Confrontaion between Disbelief and Faith

From the inception of the noble Mission, the faithful, infidels, and hypocrites were at odds. Yet, the boundaries separating these three factions had never been as stark and explicit as they were during Ashura. The hypocrisy and malicious intent of the hypocrites had never been as overtly announced as it was during Yazid the son of Muawiya's era. Past disputes among these three parties at pivotal junctures in the Islamic history, post the passing away of the Prophet (p), failed to reveal the true character, strength, intent and motivation of each group. This ambiguity posed a significant challenge to the common individual, making it arduous to discern the truth from falsehood, or to distinguish the front of faith from those of the hypocrites and infidels.

During the reign of Imam Ali (as), many of those with tainted hearts were present within his ranks. Even though they were under his rule, they failed to recognize him as a divinely appointed Imam whose orders were to be obeyed by all. Such individuals were also found in the ranks of Muawiya ibn Abu Sufyan, the leader of the forces of falsehood within the Islamic community. Thus, distinguishing the faithful from the hypocrites within Imam Ali's (as) ranks required divine inspiration or a keen sense of discernment.

This occurred because Islamic territories with all their complexities and challenges, were bequeathed to Imam Ali following the uprising against the third Caliph. This marked the initiation of a purification phase to clear the path of truth. It was necessary to manifest the divine proof (*hujja*) to people and make the essence of the true faith known.

By the time Imam Hussein (as) assumed the Imamate and the decisive standoff in Ashura was reached, the various camps had become clearly identifiable. Truth and faith were crystal clear, and anyone examining Imam Hussein's camp during this period would have no difficulty recognizing them. The same clarity was seen in the opposing camp. The presence of hypocrisy and unsound hearts was unmistakable, and at this juncture, there was no ambiguity regarding the underlying dynamics of this critical confrontation.

Interestingly, it was not the defiant infidels who posed the gravest threat to the Islamic message and path. Often, they were defeated and driven away due to their hostile and resistant nature that robbed them of the strength needed to confront faith, a fact eloquently articulated in the Holy Quran: "If the faithless fight you, they will turn their backs [to flee]. Then they will not find any protector or helper."[18]

Due to the nature of the obstinate infidels' camp and the circumstances of these hostile protesters, they lacked the strength to confront faith, resulting in frequent defeat. However, the internal conflicts and confrontations between faith and hypocrisy made it challenging for truth seekers to distinguish between truth and falsehood, and faith from disbelief, unless the positions and confrontations were significant, clear, and prominent - like when all faith rises to confront all hypocrisy (disbelief). Furthermore, the intensity of a conflict and its ensuing results hinge heavily on the clarity of each front's identity. The more transparent the motives, objectives, intentions, and dedication, the fiercer the conflict will be. Support and aid from seekers of faith and truth are contingent upon the presence of a pure, clearly discernible embodiment of faith, a factor that draws them in and motivates them to fight on the side of the faithful, thereby bolstering its strength.

However, if this condition is unmet and the image of faith remains blurred, they will end up being perplexed, non-supportive, and hesitant onlookers, depriving the faithful of the much-needed additional force for victory.

Such deficiencies in the faithful front result in these bystanders remaining historical spectators, stalling the progress of the Message, and preventing it from becoming a definitive proof (*hujja*) for the worlds.

Regrettably, this has been a recurring theme throughout the history of Islamic experience.

If one scrutinizes present-day societies, it's clear that the majority of Muslims are ready to rally behind the truth once they recognize it. The vast are naturally inclined towards the front of truth and faith, yearning to reach and support it. However, they often find themselves unable to discern its light, as it's too feeble to reach them, unless there's a significant showdown between the faithful and their adversaries. During such conflicts, which the world sporadically witnesses, this light intensifies and reaches these Islamic regions. That is until hypocrites succeed in quenching it or curbing its impact when the initial enthusiasm with which Muslims engaged in conflict wanes.

Ashura represents one of these pivotal conflicts. It unveiled pure faith and absolute truth, and unmasked the hypocrites lurking within the Islamic community. It also highlighted the potential consequences for those who choose to remain neutral, and fail to decide which front to support.

There have always been bystanders in historical confrontations, and Imam Hussein's uprising was no exception. However, divine laws dictate that remaining a neutral bystander is not an indefinite option. There will come a time when the bystander will be compelled to make a clear stance, and decide which front they belong to. This moment will come when they witness the confrontation between pure, unblemished faith and blatant disbelief. At this point, neutrality ceases to exist. A stance must be taken, and excuses about an inability to clearly identify true faith, or about the faithful failing to provide a clear path to follow, will be dismissed.

This is Allah's overarching rule that governs human life. At all times, there must be a clash, a turmoil, a confrontation that elucidates the reality of faith and its call, and delineates the path which Prophet Mohammad charted for the salvation of humanity.

Ashura was one of the most prominent milestones of the significant confrontation between faith and disbelief, the latter often masquerading in the garb of Islam, professing faith and jihad in Allah's name! Many of those who stood against Imam Hussein (as) in Ashura where among those who fought under the banner of spreading Islam worldwide. However, their true nature was unveiled in Ashura, making it clear that they were not propagating Islam or faith; rather, they were wielding their swords to present a distorted representation of Islam to humanity.

> "When Imam Hussein, peace be upon him, was martyred, people in Syria approached Yazid, presenting him with news and receiving rewards from the wealth for this. Among the matters they presented to him was the narrative of this day being a day of blessings, suggesting that people should shift from grief, weeping, tragedy, and sorrow to joy, happiness, blessings, and preparedness. May Allah judge between us and them."[19]
> Imam al-Ṣadiq(a)

Their true faces had to be unmasked so that the people, truth seekers, and those seeking salvation would understand that the path to Islamic salvation is not as these people propose. This revelation also ensured the preservation of the definitive divine proof (hujja) for all of humanity.

Had the confrontation in Karbala not occurred, our understanding of the camp of truth and the front of faith would have remained shrouded in confusion. We would have risked losing the most vital principle of this front, which is the principle of reform through advocating virtue and prohibiting vice.

The Mystery of Weeping for Imam Hussein

Throughout human history, no episode or saga equals the persistence and presence of Imam Hussein's uprising, nor matches the vast influence and depth of Ashura and its ability to inspire. The enduring legacy of Hussein stems from a secret tied to humanity's earliest beginnings on this earth. Those who quest for immortality will find it through Imam Hussein alone.

The human journey back to Allah commenced when Adam (as), as per the traditions, put his hand on his forehead, grieving for his descent to this desolate and remote earth. In that moment, Adam taught us how to seek our return to Allah through tears.

Yet, the potency of this weeping didn't fully reveal itself until the appearance of Imam Hussein, the martyr whose memory is forever associated with tears. Through his uprising and the immense tragedy that unfolded, he provided every reason for our tears. Imam Hussein awakened our dormant sorrows, transforming them into torrents of rebellion that surged from our very core. If even a few of these heart-rending tears can guide us back to Allah, then what about these floods!? Undoubtedly, the journey home to Allah will be hastened.

Allah desires and cherishes our tears. Yet, from a historical perspective, the power of weeping lies in its enduring ability to command attention. Consider how Lady Fatima mourned, and question why she cried as she did. It was certainly not an act of pretense. Her weeping was an expression of resistance, defiance, and deep sorrow for the unfolding events. News of her tears spread throughout the Muslim community, the same community that heard the Prophet proclaim, "Whoever angers her angers me, and whoever angers me has angered Allah."

Her ceaseless weeping sparked curiosity about its cause. Lady Fatima's tears were not borne out of personal whims or private matters, but from divine fury. Hence, her weeping shed light on the significant flaws that had crept into the Islamic nation at that time.

Chapter 10

The Main Characteristics of the Truth Front

When the faithful embarked on their sacred struggle to uphold Allah's path, Allah proclaimed their identity and painted for us a vivid portrait of who they truly were. True believers seek to reshape the world by extinguishing vices and promoting virtue. As stated, "You are the best nation [ever] brought forth for mankind: you bid what is right and forbid what is wrong, and have faith in Allah."[20]

Allah's ideal nation, the most exalted among all, prioritizes reform at its heart. By distancing themselves from this principle, and shunning societal transformation, believers risk forsaking their identity and faith. The preservation and intensification of faith, the maintenance of the sacred bond between believers and Allah, rests on being a reformative force upholding virtue and prohibiting vice.

When society demanded reformation, false believers shied away from their responsibility, thus revealing their true nature. This revelation was accentuated as corruption seeped into the Islamic nation's most crucial positions - its leadership and government. That's why Imam Hussein (as) said: "Anyone of you who sees a tyrannical ruler crossing the borders set by Allah, disrespecting Allah's vow, contradicting the Prophet's Sunnah, and assaulting Allah's servants, yet does not object to him neither in words nor in action, then Allah will definitely treat him the same as the tyrant."

Upon Muawiya's death and Yazid's subsequent ascension, the latter made no attempts to veil his vice, an occurrence unparalleled since the passing of Prophet Mohammad (p). Here, Muslims were thrust into a situation that scrutinized their faith. It tested their commitment to the Quran and Islam. If they professed devotion to Islam, they could not neglect its most critical principle, that is, upholding virtue, prohibiting vice, and confronting corruption. This was the essence of what Imam Hussein expressed in his uprising: "I have risen only to seek reform in the nation of my grandfather, the Prophet of Allah."

This dynamic reform movement acted as a stark divide between faith and disbelief, and a test for the faith of Muslims. True believers saw a golden opportunity to exhibit their genuine faith when Imam Hussein called them to partake in the reformation of the nation, upholding virtue, and combating vice. As for the hypocrites, who were concealing their unbelief, the pretense of faith proved futile. Many hypocrites and those with tainted hearts in Iraq were compelled to make a decision to support Imam Hussein's call for reform and become true believers, or to side with vice and corruption, thus identifying as infidels.

Imam Hussein's reform movement aimed to revive this pivotal principle and bring back into light the markers of true faith, which had grown dim over the preceding years. He aspired to unveil the essence of the religion and its missionary call and remind people of the epic struggle since the rise of Islam.

He affirmed that Islam's vitality is contingent on maintaining its reformative essence, and progress hinges on Muslims fulfilling their significant role promoting virtue and prohibiting vice.

This missionary line has always relied on the pure faith of striving believers for its survival and persistence. It is a faith that must manifest in desiring reform, goodness, and virtue, and in rejecting and being repelled by vice, crime, and corruption. Imam Hussein's uprising, thus, served as a critical step toward reviving real faith by resurrecting the duty of upholding virtue and forbidding vice. In essence, Ashura aimed at rejuvenating Islam.

There is nothing more explicitly vicious and dangerous than a depraved and obscene ruler at the helm of Islamic nation. As Imam Hussein (as) said, "If Yazid ruled then Islam would be doomed."

If we really aspire to uphold virtue and prohibit vice, then we should consider every virtue and goodness on one hand, and every form of corruption and vice on the other. If we promote virtue and prohibit vice, but turn a blind eye to the gravest vice and the most important virtue, then we are but hypocrites!

Ashura was a crossroads with no escape. Everyone had to face the test, to decide whether to align with the faithful, heed Imam Hussein's call and achieve victory and success, or to lose their faith by abandoning this responsibility and turning their backs on Imam Hussein.

This was undoubtedly a formidable test, but no one could claim that it was ambiguous or unclear. However, such is not always the case in the battles between truth and falsehood, as we previously mentioned.

You may witness numerous wars and conflicts between the infidels across the world, or confrontations between the oppressed and tyrants, or the deprived and their unjust rulers in other regions. However, as these clashes are not battles between faith and disbelief, it's not straightforward to distinguish between truth and falsehood.

Herein lies the grandeur of Ashura. It redirected conflict, confrontation, jihad, and societal movement towards the right path. Ashura made it clear that without decapitating the hydra of corruption and disbelief, people cannot experience freedom and genuine goodness. It presented us with the greatest model of reform; a model that cost Imam Hussein precious blood and unmatched sacrifices. That's why Ashura became the guiding beacon, illuminating the paths of reform seekers across the globe. So, after learning about this momentous incident, can anyone disregard its lessons or remain unaffected?

As long as we remember Ashura, contemplate its message and principles, and engage with them, this path of faith will remain a beacon of guidance and a gateway to salvation.

Imam Hussein bestowed upon humanity a colossal service by pinpointing the root of its problems and tragedies, preserving the true nature of the conflict for the free peoples of the world. This service, undoubtedly, demanded from Imam Hussein sacrifices beyond words. In contrast, the hypocrites have endeavored to erase all traces of Ashura from the onset. They pursued various strategies to achieve their goal.

Initially, they celebrated their victory in Ashura in a foolish attempt to discourage public engagement with it. This act prompted people to question the nature of a victory that led to the death of the Prophet's grandson and his household and how one could revel in such tragedy. Recognizing that this celebration backfired, they sought another path to obscure the trace of Ashura. They erased it from history books and introduced laws that hindered people from recognizing its greatness. If you peruse history books penned by historians aligned with the corrupt authority, you'll find scant mention of this major event, merely stating that on the tenth of Muharram, Hussein, son of Ali, rebelled against Yazid and was slain along with his companions in a land called Karbala.

They used a group of scholars and hadith narrators to fabricate news and hadiths about ancient events that occurred on the tenth of Muharram. They invented ceremonial and recommended acts of worship (*mustahab*) for that day to divert people from reflecting on Ashura and its proceedings. That's why you find Muslims in many places around the Islamic world fasting on the tenth of Muharram in celebration of this "sacred" day!

Regrettably, in our current time, a significant number of Muslims globally don't pause to deeply ponder over one of history's pivotal episodes, an event that played a fundamental role in unveiling the truth. The act of erasing the memory of Ashura equates to blotting out the truth that Muslims require to truly comprehend their faith,

> "Indeed, whoever joins me shall be martyred, and whoever lags behind will not reach victory. Peace be upon you."[21]
> Imam Hussein (as)

and grasp the trajectory of the Islamic calling and message, and to discern the events that unfolded along this path since its inception. Entire generations are being nurtured within these environments, devoid of even the slightest awareness of Ashura. Information about Ashura arrives as a startling revelation to them. It is disheartening that they are not permitted to know that a confrontation took place between the Prophet's grandson and the governing powers of that time!

Chapter 11

The Cascade of Atrocities Stemming from Ashura's Forgotten Lesson

The overthrow of Palestine, the agony of displacement inflicted on its people, and the most horrific crimes committed against them, all represent a continuing chain of horrors, disasters, and woes endured by Muslims following the martyrdom of Imam Hussein and the captivity of the women from the chosen Prophet's (as) lineage.

As Muslims begin to understand the interconnection between the Palestinian issue and other pivotal events in Islamic history realizing that their struggles echo the trials of those who came before them, all the way back to the seminal event of Ashura, they will uncover the true roots of these calamities and tragedies. Only then will they discover their path to liberation.

Chapter 12

The Interplay of Intellect and
Emotions in Karbala

The incident of Ashura has invoked a diverse range of responses. Some Muslims have had their lives profoundly shaped by this event, while it went unnoticed by some other Muslims. Between these two extremes lies another group. This group has not dismissed Ashura as many have done, and could not ignore such a momentous event. To them, Ashura signifies a grave historical calamity. However, their engagement, sadly, remains largely emotional. They are content with mourning the family of Imam Hussein as if grieving for a departed relative. Their emotional interaction is limited to holding condolence gatherings. After these sessions, they dry their tears and resume their usual life rhythm.

Such Muslims have failed to comprehend the true depth of this tragedy and its dimensions, viewing it merely as heartbreaking incidents of murder and captivity. If they had pondered upon the status, character, and motives of the one who was slain in Karbala, the nature and intentions of the slayer, and the causes and aims of this confrontation, their tears wouldn't have stopped at a few drops. Instead, they would have transformed into floods capable of toppling the thrones of oppressors, regardless of their identities!

This lack of contemplation about the event, and the absence of intellectual engagement with Imam Hussein's uprising, has reduced their emotional interaction to a bare minimum, failing to incite the kind of action and responsiveness that Imam Hussein had hoped for.

In conclusion, it is anticipated that those who engage both emotionally and intellectually with the uprising of Imam Hussein will be the ones who will tread its path, for the intellect grasps the truth, understands its dimensions, and extracts its meanings and facts, what will fill the heart and emotions with innumerable motives to move, interact, respond, and be ready for sacrifice. Ultimately, this interaction will reach its peak, and individuals will choose to walk the path of Imam Hussein, a path of reform, promoting virtue, and denouncing vice. It's a journey that demands great sacrifices, the greatest of which is laying down one's life for the sake of Allah.

Chapter 13

Ashura: The Clarion Call for Righteous Leadership and Equitable Imamate

The essence of Islam and the roadmap to human salvation lies in the belief in Allah. Genuine faith is a mindful connection with the source of all that is virtuous, perfect, and capable in existence; that is, Allah. The integration of such faith in a community signifies that it has tapped into the real source of a prosperous, happy, and capable life. This is why embedding the pillars of faith in a community forms the primary objective of the Islamic message and of all prophets.

A community that earnestly believes in Allah and maintains a strong connection with Him is fully cognizant of the values, virtues, and beauty that faith imparts in life. Such a consciousness makes the community extremely responsive to any forms of ugliness, vice, or corruption. To believe in Allah is to believe in all that is good and perfect. In essence, it is a faith in virtue and a rejection of vice, as the heart of a believer can never be complacent or tolerant towards vice, injustice, and ugliness.

Believing in Allah is the ultimate purifier of all contaminants and the most prized quality that a heart may possess. Thus, faith is best expressed through the pursuit of virtue and avoidance of vice. Virtue represents a good life, a fine and beautiful environment, and all that is aesthetically pleasing. Conversely, vice embodies all that is wrong, corrupt, and unpleasant whether at an individual level, within the natural and environmental sphere, or pertaining to social or political life.

Yazid, as an individual and as an authority, represented the most grotesque image of a leader and societal head, as he championed and legitimized depravity and acclimated society to it. This predicament made the rebellion against Yazid an imperative for maintaining faith in Allah. For anyone who accepts Yazid and his deeds will soon find their faith waning if it ever existed. The coexistence of two diametrically opposite elements within a single heart is impossible, as Allah asserted: "Allah has not put two hearts within any man."[22]

Conversely, striving for virtue, encompassing all that is beautiful, fine, and good, is also a prerequisite for sustaining faith. There is no doubt that the epitome of virtue in societal life and the lives of communities lies in having a virtuous individual at the helm; someone who personifies and champions all forms of perfection, guides the community towards them, lays the foundation for institutions dedicated to this cause, and reinforces them through the implementation of programs, laws, and legislations.

Therefore, advocating for the existence of a just and virtuous Imam, and encouraging people to follow and obey him is the paramount virtue to uphold.

Just as rejecting vice primarily manifests through the repudiation of tyrants and corrupt, unjust governments, endorsing virtue fundamentally exhibits through the community's collective endeavour towards virtues and perfection, achievable only under the stewardship of a virtuous leader who is the embodiment of all virtues.

Thus, Imam Hussein's uprising is a call for the righteous Imamate and the virtuous leadership. Anyone who comprehends the essence of this uprising and its objectives clearly understands that the path of Imam Hussein, which is the path of messengers and prophets, is the route of the Islamic message that guides and directs humanity towards the establishment of a just government.

Those who regard themselves as followers of Imam Hussein, who love him and mourn his tragedy, but fail to grasp the concept of governance, are fundamentally misinterpreting Ashura and Imam Hussein's uprising.

The path of the Islamic message, which ensures the happiness, progress, and prosperity of humanity, is fundamentally symbolized in the establishment of a just and good government. Achieving this goal requires first the eradication of the tyrannical, corrupt, and unjust party that oppresses people and forcefully governs them through money, coercion, and suppression.

«Whoever hears our call, we the people of the Prophet's household, and then does not respond to us, Allah will cast them face-first into the fire of Hell.»[23]
Imam Hussein (as)

The first major lesson imparted by Imam Hussein's uprising is that Imam Hussein rose to establish Allah's governance on earth, regardless of whether this objective is realized in his era or in the future. Hence, implementing religion and its virtues and values in social life necessitates that a society's politics and leadership are righteous and virtuous.

Chapter 14

How Do We Take the Path of
Ashura

Once we comprehend that Ashura and Imam Hussein's uprising are extensions of the Prophet's message, and we discern the connection between this uprising and the Prophet's mission, we get a step closer to grasping the events that unfolded between the Islamic mission and the tenth of Muharram in the year 61 AH. This understanding enables us to appreciate the trajectory of Islamic history, from the genesis and propagation of Islam, through its metamorphoses, the experiences of Muslims, to our present circumstances. It equips us with the ability to ascertain our current position, whether we desire to be at the forefront of truth and reform, and if we wish to be authentic followers of Imam Hussein.

Imam Hussein's uprising, rich in stance and principle, augments our understanding of not only Islam's journey since its dawn but also many of our contemporary issues.. It empowers us to make informed decisions at crucial times. Thus, those who follow the path of Imam Hussein will find his uprising an inspiration to take the right stance.

The first message Ashura delivers is that loyalty to and affiliation with Imam Hussein's uprising have come to distinguish the righteous from the followers of falsehood. This distinction holds severe implications as it delineates not merely categories of people in this life but also the fate of souls in the hereafter. It demarcates those who succeed from those who fail, and those who earn Allah's blessings from those who invite His wrath. Real Islam and genuine faith align with Imam Hussein's path. Only an Islam that resonates with Imam Hussein's uprising and path is acceptable to Allah.

Numerous hadiths clarify the line of demarcation drawn by Imam Hussein and the path of Ashura, distinguishing those who side with the truth and those who align with falsehood. As for those on the fence, their neutrality will be short-lived. They will be called to account for their stance on the tragedy of Karbala. Sooner or later, one must choose a side, as neutrality cannot be perpetual.

Consequently, a believer feels irresistibly drawn to Imam Hussein's cause, viewing it as the central and most significant cause in their life, irrespective of the time that has elapsed since this uprising. After all, how can one remain neutral or ignorant of their primary responsibility in life after learning about the confrontation in Karbala, where absolute truth faced absolute falsehood?

As such, those who are ignorant and oppose to the truth have always endeavoured to erase the events and principles of Imam Hussein's uprising, aware of the profound impact it has on one's life and major decisions. Upon understanding the truth about Ashura, one finds themselves in a battlefield akin to that of Karbala, faced with the stark divide between truth and falsehood, faith and disbelief. At this juncture, a decision must be made: either align with the present-day «Hussein» or join the opposing camp. 

This is encapsulated in the saying, «Every day is Ashura, and every land is Karbala.» As long as falsehood, tyranny, injustice, and disbelief prevail in this world, the confrontation persists, even if the ignorant are oblivious to it. Their detachment from real events and preoccupation with trivial matters such as sports and entertainment festivals has shielded them from studying history and reflecting on its lessons. The world today, as in the past, continues this struggle. Every rational person must identify and join the front of truth, represented by Imam Hussein, in the present time.

As we contemplate the various events and reflect upon

what transpired on the tenth of Muharram, we must not linger in indecision or uncertainty regarding our course of action. It becomes clear who represents the camp of truth and its adherents, and likewise, who aligns with the camp of falsehood and its allies.

> "By Allah, I would wish to be slain, then revived, then slain again, and so on, a thousand times over, so that Allah may utilize such a sacrifice to avert death from you and from these young souls of your household."[24]
> Zuhayr ibn al-Qayn

In this way, Imam Hussein's camp extends throughout history. There is always a Husseini call and uprising, taking place in different locations and times, offering a timeless example for us to follow, delineating the divine path we can tread no matter where we are.

To strengthen our bond with Imam Hussein and his uprising and principles, which embody the core principles of Islam, religious leaders and Imams of Islam have taken great care to express this through a variety of deeds, movements, activities, and acts of worship.

We come to realize the significance of a vital set of worship practices, where Imam Hussein's presence resonates within our prayers, permeates our daily lives, and holds great significance in the most crucial moments we encounter. For instance, it is recommended to prostrate on Imam Hussein's soil during prayer and to use it for healing purposes. This soil has been employed as a remedy for ages, proving its efficacy in treating complex and intractable diseases. In addition to that, we cannot overlook the numerous blessings that individuals experience when visiting Imam Hussein, standing by his revered grave, and seeking intercession beneath his sacred dome. The remarkable and overwhelming number of pilgrims who flock to his shrine during various occasions, such as the month of Ramadan, holidays, and blessed nights, signifies that Imam Hussein is an ever-present figure in every significant event of our lives.

This is the divine approach advocated by the Ahl al-Bayt to establish a strong bond and connection with Imam Hussein, ensuring that his cause remains vibrant and influential in our lives and consciousness. The exemplary model demonstrated on the tenth of Muharram over a thousand years ago should resonate and be manifested in every aspect and facet of our life. To embody the true spirit of Imam Hussein and to reap the blessings he offers in our social, personal, worldly, and spiritual endeavors, our relationship with him should be rooted in comprehending his revolution, embracing it wholeheartedly, and actively working towards its application and perpetuation.

Imam Hussein's Ashura serves as a guiding principle, a path, and a way of life, as long as the struggle between truth and falsehood continues, and as long as there is an oppressor and an oppressed. No matter where oppression is encountered, there is no inspiration, aid, motivation, or catalyst for rebellion stronger than Imam Hussein's uprising and Ashura.

Ashura, a school of rebellion and rejection of oppression, of life reform and societal advancement, provides reformers with the lessons they need to stay on the right path, the motivations that bolster their determination, and the spirit that encourages great sacrifices. Its encompassment of all aspects of greatness in terms of message, work, jihad, sacrifice, and giving, sets it apart from any other epic in history.

Chapter 15

The Lessons from Kufa

It is evident that a notable number of the individuals who confronted Imam Hussein in Karbala, attacked his camp, and committed the most atrocious crimes against him were those who had initially fought alongside the camp of truth during the time of Imam Ali. Amid the chaos of that trajic day, these traitorous forces initiated the onslaught before the arrival of the Sham army, renowned for its affiliation to the camp of falsehood.

A considerable number of individuals who engaged in battle against Imam Hussein had previously fought in the army of his father, the Imam, or had direct experience with it. The question arises: How did these individuals transition from fighting alongside the righteous Imam to fighting against him? And could such a transition occur in our present time?

The fabric of any party is woven from the threads of affiliation and allegiance, and not merely by religious or sectarian labels it carries. The presumption that the populace was segregated into Shias and Sunnis is misguided. Rather, the primary demarcations were allegiance to either the righteous Imam or the corrupt tyrant. Within the camp of the righteous Imam, one could find individuals whose presence was not driven by true allegiance. Such was the case with a majority in Imam Ali's camp, many of whom did not align with him because he was Allah's appointed infallible Imam and Prophet Mohammad's rightful successor. This was starkly revealed when the time came for these individuals to demonstrate their loyalty, and many turned against him, exposing their true affiliations.

A pivotal challenge faced by Imam Ali was that many of his inherited soldiers were oblivious to his esteemed position and value as an infallible Imam. This ignorance prevailed amongst those who fought alongside him in the battles of

Siffin, Nahrawan, and Jamal. The concept of divine Imamate had been neglected during the quarter-century reign of the three caliphs, leading to the emergence of generations unfamiliar with it. This inevitably triggered a resurgence of tribal affiliations and allegiances, becoming the primary influence on societal activity, even if it involved battling for the propagation of Islam.

Imam Ali's brief reign, lasting no more than five years, teemed with challenges that threatened the very existence of Islam and the Message. These obstacles hindered him from establishing the notion of Imamate and the divine guardianship, known as Wilayah. Consequently, the majority of the community remained distant from comprehending the requisite allegiance. For example, an individual could associate with Imam Ali by merely fighting alongside him, even without understanding his spiritual position, role, rank of faith, and divine esteem.

When battles and affiliations are detached from this divine guardianship, or wilayah, secular, personal, and tribal interests swiftly dominate one's character and actions. Some fought beside Imam Ali, not for the religion and the Message, but out of self-interest, mirrored during the reign of the third caliph, whose kin monopolized the Muslim treasury, igniting the rage of the Islamic nation leading to a rebellion against Othman, resulting in his death.

Subsequently, when many pledged allegiance to Imam Ali, it was not due to his divine appointment but rather because of his incorruptibility, his familial ties to the Prophet, and his opposition to the third caliph. Only a minority truly grasped Imam Ali's spiritual, moral, and religious position. Thus, most allegiances were dictated by secular considerations and interests, with scant regard to faith in Allah and personal affairs viewed through the lens of faith This implies the importance of recognizing the need for divine intervention and acknowledging its value. However, many have lost sight of the divine and faithful aspects of their lives. If these individuals had based their allegiance and loyalty on truth and faith, they would have recognized the necessity of having a flawless and infallible Imam in their lives. They would have strived to support and follow him. Faith teaches us that Allah's definite proof (*hujjah*) to his servants is only complete with the existence of a just Imam.

The understanding and knowledge we have today about the concept of Imamate were not widely known or disseminated during that period. Only a select few faithful individuals sought knowledge from the pure source of religion. This ignorance was exploited by Muawiya and later Yazid to sway allegiance towards them, resulting in a horrific shift of loyalty most brutally evident in Karbala.

This provides us with a profound lesson for the present. If we wish to comprehend the fate of any faction, we must scrutinize the nature of the allegiance held by its members, prioritizing their convictions and beliefs over emotional ties. A faction may profess emotional ties to the pure infallible Ahl Al-Beit, but lack proper conviction in their divine Imamate and guardianship, supporting the Imam's reign merely to defy others. Such an emotionally charged faction can, at any given moment, become a weapon wielded by the enemy against the Imam and the path of wilayah and faith.

Unless a faction of truth and rebellion is grounded in an understanding of Imamate and divine guardianship, it harbors within itself the seeds of its downfall, defenceless against the possibility of perpetrating heinous historical crimes, much like those that unfolded in Karbala.

In a divine orchestration, the events of Karbala played out between Imam Hussein and the people of Kufa and Iraq, ending before Yazid's Sham army arrived. This highlighted the internal nature of the problem, laying bare the fragility of the camp that was once the beacon of truth. The concept of allegiance conversion was thus elucidated, enabling contemplation of its reasons and preventative measures.

The real awareness of the issues of Imamate and divine guardianship, or wilayah, is manifested as follows:

1. Individuals must have faith in Allah's presence and guidance in their lives, and His governance over societies and political powers.

2. They must acknowledge that the infallible just Imam is the epitome of divine care, upbringing, and humanity's management.

3. Such belief must translate into life as loyalty and submission to this Imam, working under his banner, serving him and his message, and engaging in jihad in his camp.

Imam Hussein, through his uprising, aimed to highlight these crucial aspects. Unfortunately, many who empathize with Ashura fail to grasp this essence, misconstruing the events of Karbala as a Shia-Sunni conflict. This misunderstanding is fuelled by divisive forces aiming to instigate discord among Muslims along Sunni-Shiite lines.

Retracing the history to the time of Ashura, one would not find any Sunni labelling, as Sunni factions had not yet been established. The divisions within the Muslim community were based on politics and allegiances. The individuals who prayed and performed ablution in the camp of Umar ibn Saad followed the same practices as the companions of Imam Hussein. There were no significant differences in the legal rulings observed by both camps, unlike the divergences that emerged among different Islamic sects later on. Their beliefs were also not fundamentally different. The conflict in Karbala did not revolve around theological debates such as predestination or free will, the creation or revelation of the Quran, the unity of divine attributes and essence, or other theological issues that later caused disagreements among Muslims.

The battles in Karbala were not over doctrinal issues, nor were they influenced by the controversial incident of Saqifa post-Prophet Ahl Al-Beits death regarding his rightful successor.

Motivated by greed and fear of Yazid's army, the Kufa camp took arms against Imam Hussein. This was primarily due to their ignorance of divine guardianship, or wilayah. The absence of belief in Imamate and wilāyah empowered these base motivations, causing them to ignore Imam Hussein's pleas.

Similar conversions and atrocities can occur in any faction or society claiming emotional bonds with the immaculate Imams or Imam Mahdi. Loyalty begins with understanding Imamate, experiencing it, and integrating it into everyday life. This is the only safeguard against becoming akin to the Kufa people who slaughtered the Imam of their time.

In a perplexing paradox, many collectives today organize commemorations for Imam Hussein (as), feigning sorrow and echoing his call, while simultaneously bending their knee to despots and enemies of the divine message. It's distressing when the remembrance of Ashura and Imam Hussein's uprising becomes a tool for erasing its very principles, muffling its voice, distorting its essence, and silencing those who yearn for change and reform.

For the commemoration of Ashura to truly inspire, it must begin where Imam Hussein began. This immaculate, martyred Imam aimed to enlighten all around him that his rebellion was for a divine purpose, a mission appointed by Allah. Certainly, there were individuals who held affection for the Imam and empathized with his plight, yet they lacked the crucial understanding that he was an Imam designated by Allah and did not grasp his spiritual, moral, and divine reverence.

"By Allah, if I knew that I would be killed, then revived, then burnt, then revived, then scattered, and that this would happen to me seventy times over, I would not abandon you until I met my end defending you. And why would I not do so? For it is but a single martyrdom, followed by an enduring honor that will never cease."[25]
Muslim ibn Awsajah

This ignorance manifested in their interactions with him. Instead of seeking his counsel on divine edicts, they engaged in disputes with him, exposing a prevailing lack of knowledge concerning divine caliphate, imamate, and the essence of true faith.

A poet from the era of Imam Hussein, Farazdaq, encapsulated the relationship between the people of Kufa and Imam Hussein with his words: «Their hearts were with him, but their swords were against him.» This aptly underscores that an emotional connection devoid of genuine allegiance can horrifyingly lead one to harm their beloved.

The principle of imamate and belief in it was not widely understood in the early years of the Message and until Imam Hussein's time. During this period, the faithful were grappling to establish the necessary groundwork that would facilitate a deeper understanding of the concept of imamate. Ashura was a significant milestone in this journey, and we witness the monumental role this great uprising played in this arena.

Today, we are no longer divided on the basis of interests, or on the basis of the oppressor and the oppressed. Instead, we should align ourselves on the battleground between faith and unbelief, between divine guardianship and tyrannical rule, thereby distinguishing the true oppressor from the genuinely oppressed.

Those who are educated in the school of Ashura are best equipped to comprehend history through the lens of Allah's presence and planning. As such, they stand a chance to summon true faith at the forefront of major confrontations and struggles. And how direly we need the realization that life itself is a doctrine and a holy struggle, or jihad!

Chapter 16

When Martyrdom Overcame the
Might of Swords

A careful study of the aims of the two primary factions in Imam Hussein's uprising, and a thoughtful reflection on the events following Ashura, reveals the stark contrasts between the victorious and the defeated.

The first faction aimed to rekindle a societal reform movement. Given the circumstances of the era, this could only be achieved through the willingness to shed blood, embrace martyrdom for the divine cause, and withstand the tribulations of captivity. Through its sacrifice and divine struggle, this faction met its objective and, without a doubt, emerged victorious in this confrontation.

In contrast, the second faction sought to install a royal, hereditary tribal rule, undermine Islamic values, propagate ignorance and tyranny, and subjugate Muslims. They failed to realize these goals. Hence, despite their apparent dominance on the tenth of Muharram, they were indeed the defeated.

In any confrontation, the parameters of victory and defeat are measured by these standards. Survival does not equate to victory, as no one is granted eternal life. During that period, both Imam Hussein and Yazid were destined to pass away, as no one can remain in this world indefinitely. True victory lies in realizing one's objectives, even if one is physically absent. A contemplation of Ashura and its aftermath makes it abundantly clear who the genuine victor was.

One crucial result of this confrontation was the delegitimization of Yazid's rule and the Umayyad dynasty. Ashura unmasked Yazid, revealing him as nothing more than a base criminal. He consequently lost his primary means of bolstering his rule — his spurious claim to legitimacy via his asserted connection to the Prophet as his successor.

Muslim rulers often flaunted their title of «Caliph», the Prophet's successor, in an attempt to convince Muslims of the legitimacy of their rule. However, Yazid's heinous crime of killing Imam Hussein severed his link to the Prophet, making it challenging for him to fill the shoes of the caliph. Over time, the Umayyad government gradually lost its legitimacy, leading to its ultimate downfall.

Imam Zein Al-Abedin pinpointed the real victor when he declared, «O Yazid, when you hear the call of adhan, you will know which one of us is victorious.» This is because the adhan proclaims, «I testify that Mohammad is the Messenger of Allah" universally; in Sham and beyond. As long as the Prophet's name resonates, no ruler who persecutes Allah's Prophet and blatantly opposes him can claim victory. Consequently, the stage was set for revolts and rebellions across the Islamic world against those who slaughtered the Prophet's descendants and captured his women.

The Prophet (as) has consistently remained the most revered figure in the collective conscience of Muslims throughout the ages. Utilizing this reverence to promote the principles and values of this great missionary figure is crucial. It is impossible to be a Muslim and harbor disdain for the greatest Prophet. Hence, any debate within the Islamic community concerning the Prophet should center on understanding his persona, his Sunna, role, and life journey. Direct attacks on the Prophet, as committed by Yazid, were categorically rejected, turning the perpetrator into a pariah within the Muslim community. This marked a significant triumph for Ahl-Albeit, a victory made possible by the Ashura uprising.

Yazid foolishly assumed he could perpetrate such an atrocious crime against Allah's Prophet and Islam's leader without eliciting a response from the Muslim community. Disregarding his father's counsel to refrain from harming Imam Hussein publicly and directly, Yazid demolished the mainstay of the Umayyad government that sought to eradicate Islam and its values.

Imam Hussein's teachings highlight that true victory lies in upholding values and virtues within society. He emphasized that the significance of life does not solely rely on living a few additional days compared to others. Rather, true victory is attained by sacrificing oneself in the path of God, reviving noble values, and defending them. When we grasp the genuine essence of life and death, we can comprehend the true meaning of triumph and defeat. Thus, it becomes clear to us who emerges as the ultimate victor on the day of Ashura.

Ashura: The Eternal Echo from the Dawn of Time

In the Holy Quran, Allah says, "Say: My Lord would not concern Himself with you but for your prayer."[26] This verse has been interpreted in numerous ways, with one well-known interpretation suggesting that Allah does not heed His creation unless they approach Him with prayers and needs. However, another perspective to consider is that if Allah Almighty had not called you to Him, He would not have bestowed His care upon you. This divine beckoning towards Allah is the very lifeblood of humanity's existence, survival, and progression. For, Allah would not maintain humanity unless there was a potential for it to gravitate towards Him.

The crux of a prophet's mission lies in summoning people towards Allah. But when prophets felt despair in achieving this objective among their people they beseeched Allah to obliterate their people. The trust reached our Prophet Muhammad, peace be upon him, and he was tasked with calling humanity to Allah as well. Yet, being the embodiment of Allah's all-encompassing mercy, he couldn't countenance the destruction of humanity post his demise. He yearned to safeguard all of mankind, despite the enormity of the required sacrifices.

However, the cost was steep. He needed to forge individuals in his likeness; successors who would carry on his work, protect humanity, and simultaneously be prepared for their sacrifice - they were to be subjected to torment and death. Furthermore, the Prophet had to pronounce his readiness to witness his women taken captive, all for the sake of preserving the divine call till the end of time. This monumental task fell upon the shoulders of the Prophet's grandson, Imam Hussein, to carry forth this trust and safeguard the Earth and its people.

The task bequeathed to Imam Hussein was not merely the preservation of humans in their most primal, animalistic sense, but the ideal of man who, despite facing threats and challenges, remains true to his innate nature (*fitrah*). As the verse goes, "The nature made by Allah in which He has made men; there is no altering of Allah's creation; that is the right religion."

A contemplation of Imam Hussein's life, actions, and biography reveals a singular truth: they are irrevocably tied to Karbala. From his pre-birth, childhood, and until his martyrdom, the discourse has always revolved around Karbala. As it is said, "O Hussein, you possess a divine esteem that can only be attained through martyrdom."

After the martyrdom of Imam Ali, Imam Hussein did not initiate any significant or notable movement. The reason? To ensure that Ashura does not become merely a chapter in his life or a stage in the preservation of the faith. By focusing on the incident at Tuff, he sought to underscore that Karbala was the sum total of his existence, and all his efforts came to a standstill until the tenth day of Muharram.

Comprehending Imam Hussein's role is crucial to understanding the significance of Karbala, to fathom its dimensions, and to discern the true Islamic path. The life of Imam Hussein, the impeccable Imam and the perfect man, does not comprise numerous intervals, with his journey to Karbala and his martyrdom being a mere episode. Instead, his life is an embodiment of the uprising of Ashura, and nothing else.

Chapter 17

The Quintessence of Timing

One of the cardinal teachings of Ashura emphasizes the criticality of assuming the right position at the opportune moment. Ashura serves as a potent reminder that a failure to take appropriate action at the right time can pave the way for significant setbacks, if not outright calamities. This lesson is underscored in the events that followed Ashura, where those who lagged in rallying behind Imam Hussein (as) later faced distress, humiliation, and persecution. Their lives were ravaged, and many of them lost their faith and hereafter. Numerous individuals were acquainted with Imam Hussein (as) and were aware of his noble virtue. They recognized his call as just, knew of Yazid's debauched nature, and understood that his rule over the Muslim community could spell the downfall of Islam. Yet, history illuminates how they faltered, procrastinated, and were hesitant in their response when the Imam rose and sought their assistance. More disconcerting was how their reluctance heavily influenced a large segment of onlookers, who, at the pivotal juncture, sided with Yazid instead of aligning with the truth.

Such an outcome is the result of hesitancy and indecision amongst those who ought to be at the forefront, which can spur others to take an opposing course. Merely voicing doubts by the elite and leaders in any society can nudge the masses towards the precipice. Subsequently, the despotic ruler unleashes persecution and suppression on the waverers, lest they awaken their dormant conscience and consciousness. Consequently, they suffer losses in this world and the hereafter.

To grasp the severity of their predicament, one must examine the importance and gravity of the matter over which they wavered. Ashura was not a sudden, unexpected occurrence; it was the culmination of an extended series of events that led to this standoff. These developments allowed any observer or bystander ample opportunity to define their position. Therefore, the dilemma was not about awareness or knowledge, but about seizing the right stance at the crucial moment. For, one may be aware of the facts, yet falter when the time comes to take the necessary action.

Some people overlook the fact that life presents tests and challenges that require prior preparation to be able to adopt the right stance when needed. The disregard of such a crucial matter stems from neglecting the importance of Allah Almighty.

Those who are acquainted with Allah, glorified and exalted, recognize His omnipresence in all aspects of life, particularly in crucial matters. It is beyond doubt that Allah Almighty does not overlook significant issues such as the governance and leadership of society, unlike some minor mistakes that may be forgiven. The question of government and societal leadership is intricately connected to religion and the divine message, constituting a pivotal element in the divine argument and plan. Hence, it is an exceptionally sensitive matter, and any laxity in addressing it would signify underestimating the presence of Allah Almighty. These are substantial matters in the sight of Allah. Those who revere Allah also hold these matters in high esteem and give them significant consideration. If this group truly recognizes Allah's greatness, they would understand the importance of leading a society and would consistently be prepared and actively engaged in its endeavors and challenges. As a result, it would not catch them off guard or come as a surprise to them. Those who were taken aback by the events of Ashura and hesitated at the critical moment when they were called upon to support Imam Hussein were so due to their initial disengagement and indifference towards this issue. On

the other hand, those who work tirelessly for the sake of Allah, who honor Him, and recognize the issues He deems significant, will not require a public call to engage in these issues. Instead, they will be at the vanguard, inviting others to join them.

This lesson serves as a cautionary tale that anyone who distances themselves from significant life issues, due to a weak awareness of Allah's presence in their conscience, will be caught unawares by major tests and challenges. This surprise might incapacitate their ability to take the correct stance at the right time, leading to a fate similar to that which befell the wavering individuals post Ashura and that which many in the Islamic world face today.

The onus, therefore, lies in being mindful of the circumstances and trials that envelop us. We must reflect on them and their consequences and consider the outcome of being a mere observer, shirking responsibilities, and failing to make the right stand.

The adversaries of Islam and faith have always been active, and their numbers seem to be increasing. They possess both the capacity and the intent to demolish any environment conducive to fostering the faithful, the virtuous, the rebellious, and the free. While you may remain oblivious to this scenario, they are not. They conspire relentlessly to dismantle your community, your environment, and the faith-filled ambience around you. Therefore, unless you stay informed and engaged, you may face a fate similar to those who missed seizing the right stance at the crucial moment in Ashura. This is a paramount lesson that we learned from the greatest school of life.

References

1. Holy Quran 29:2
2. Amali al-Saduq, p. 111
3. Bihar al-Anwar, v. 257, p. 45
4. Tuhaf al-Uqul, p. 244
5. Nahj al-Balaghah, vol. 1, p. 502
6. Holy Quran 2:134
7. Holy Quran 3:103
8. Bihar al-Anwar, v. 304, p. 44
9. Holy Quran 72:16
10. Amali al-Saduq, p. 133
11. Tahdhib al-Ahkam, vol. 6, p. 123
12. Holy Quran 4:100
13. Holy Quran 3:133
14. Holy Quran 2:148
15. Mafatih al-Jinan, p.730
16. Tuhaf al-Uqul, p. 249
17. Holy Quran 5:48
18. Holy Quran 48:22
19. Ilal al - Sharai, p.255
20. Holy Quran 3:110
21. Basa'ir al-Darajat, p.481
22. Holy Quran 33:4
23. Amali al-Saduq, p. 137
24. Al-Irshad, p. 214
25. Al-Irshad, p. 214
26. Holy Quran 25:77

www.ingramcontent.com/pod-product-compliance
Lightning Source LLC
LaVergne TN
LVHW051454170726
843492LV00002B/677